45th Anniversary:

45 Epic Years

Our reflections, memories, thoughts and ideas for the future.

∞

Books With Soul
Somewhere in the desert, sea and forest.
www.bookswithsoul.com
∞
Books with Soul supports copyright for all authors.
Thank you for purchasing a copyrighted edition of this book.
First Edition 2018

Copyright © 2018 Anita Kaltenbaugh
Books With Soul
All rights reserved.
This book, or any portion thereof, may not be reproduced in any form without permission.
Printed in the United States of America
ISBN-13: **978-1-949325-12-6**

Life is a collection of moments
-unknown

This journal belongs to a magnificent couple who has shared
epic memories:

_____

*Inside these pages are their memories,
thoughts, inspirations and
ideas for the last 45 and the next 45 years.*

Date: _____

Given by: _____

Congratulations!

You belong in a very special club. Forty-five years together. Forty-five years of living. Forty-five years is worth celebrating. You are worth celebrating.

This book is for YOUR memories, written in your own words.

Take five minutes a day, a week or even monthly and write a simple thought.
Jot down a memory.
Write a few words.
Write down wishes.
Ideas for the future.
Anything you write will be preserved.
It only takes a minute to record a moment in time forever.

Imagine, you discovered a journal.

A journal written by a friend who passed. Perhaps, it was an aunt, uncle or grandparent whom you never met. Maybe even your mother or father or a sibling who is no longer with you. A person in your life who you miss their words and presence every day.

If they wrote a few words down from time to time, and you were able to read them and reflect back--what a gift that would be. A few words to make you remember, smile and laugh as you read their happy thoughts or favorite color.

Maybe, you have children and you want to remember their first year, or any year, and reflect on their childhood.

Maybe you want your grandchildren to get know their grandparents. Or you have unborn grandchildren, who may never understand what your life was like when they were born. How about great-grandchildren?

Maybe you want to remember your wedding day, your first trip to Europe, or your first home in a new place.

This is a place to scribble a thought a day, or even a memory a week. There are no rules.

This is a book to write a memory or a thought for the future.

Maybe no one will ever read your words--but you. And, in the future you will stumble upon this book made of paper, because it can't be lost when the computer crashes, or when our fast-paced technology changes the way we share or store data. This journal is physical and will always be around.

Maybe one day you will jot down a great quote you heard that day, and it will inspire you or someone you love in the future. Maybe you wrote down a great song, or even a favorite recipe, and your future self will thank you for it.

Maybe it's simply noting the words of your heart, your life together or your secret dreams. A glance back at the best book or movie you read this year. A glance back at your firsts.

Collect your memories.

Do what you want with this book, there's enough space for a thought a day, or one a week.
Write some words down for history, to share with others, or just to enlighten your future self.
Answer a few of the questions and write the date on each page.

Share your journey.

Write your words, together as a couple, or as individuals or both.

Hide it, share it or leave it for someone you love.

Happy 45th year anniversary.
And yes, the Best is Yet to Come.

www.bookswithsoul.com

"You can't go back and change the beginning, but you can start where you are and change the ending."

-unknown

45 years of
Marriage

540 months of moments together
2546 weeks of hugs
16,425 days of laughter
394,200 hours full of love and understanding
23,667,714 minutes of having each other's back
1,420,062,840 seconds of you and I

What I most want to remember about our 45th Anniversary celebration:

MONTH 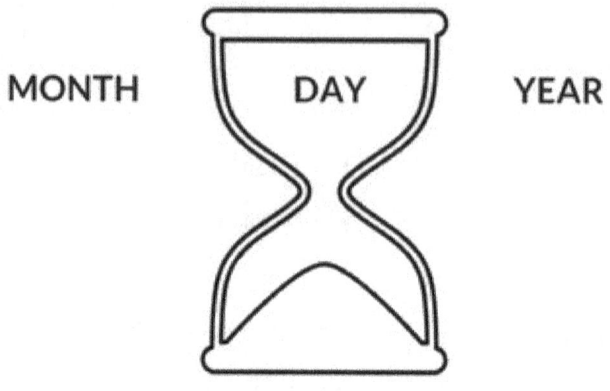 YEAR

If there is one thing I want to remember about this day it is this:

A thought or a sentence for the day:

I want to remember all the places
we have lived:

And we lived here:

Our first vacation we ever took together:

This is the destination we haven't been to yet, but I want to go:

MONTH 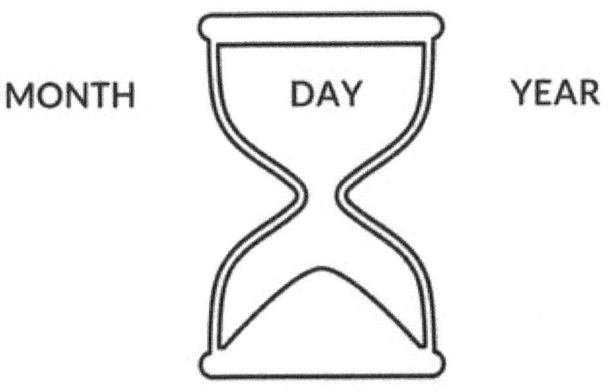 YEAR

If there is one thing I want to remember about this day it is this:

A thought or a sentence for the day:

MONTH YEAR

Here's a 1st for this year:
The first time I ever....

A thought or a sentence for the day:

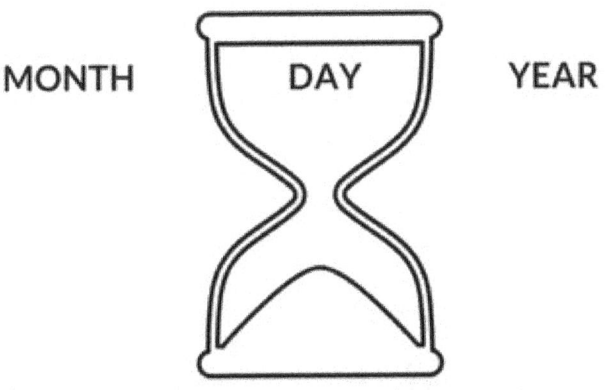

MONTH DAY YEAR

Right now, my favorite song is:

A thought or a sentence for the day:

If I had to pick a song that is our song it is:

We danced to this song at our wedding:

"To live is the rarest thing in the world. Most people exist, that is all." Oscar Wilde

My favorite quote is:

| MONTH | DAY | YEAR |

A thought or a sentence for the day:

If there is one thing I want to remember about this day it is this:

MONTH 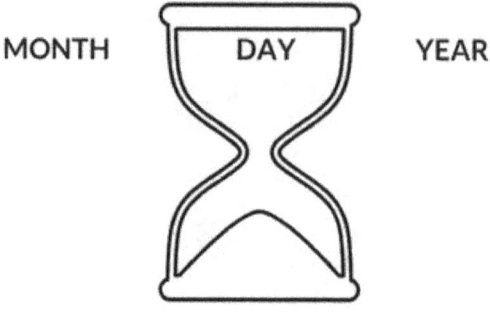 YEAR

This surprised me:

A thought or a sentence for the day:

MONTH 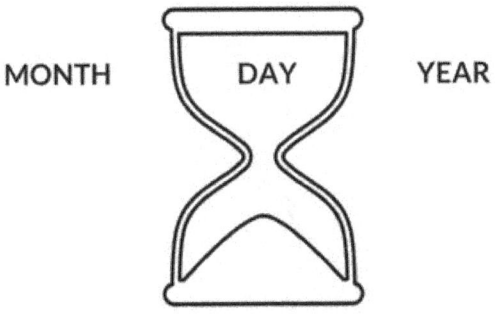 DAY   YEAR

If there is one thing I want to remember about this day it is this:

A thought or a sentence for the day:

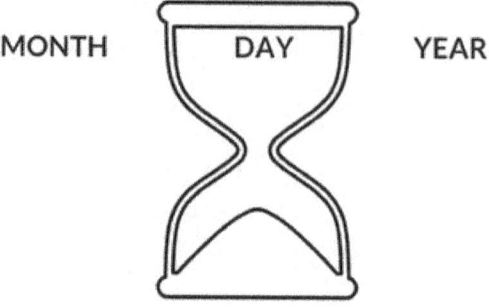

MONTH   DAY   YEAR

At this point in my life, this is my best advice for someone I love:

A thought or a sentence for the day:

The thing that most surprised me about children:

| MONTH | DAY | YEAR |

A thought or a sentence for the day:

If there is one thing I want to remember about this day it is this:

MONTH   DAY   YEAR

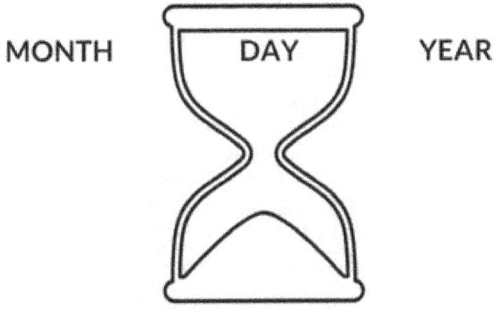

A recipe to remember or at least my favorite food of the moment:

A thought or a sentence for the day:

MONTH   DAY   YEAR

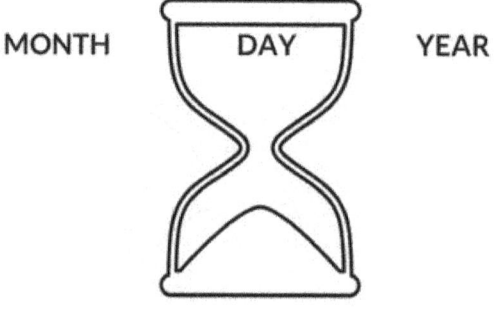

I am most amazed at this new technology:

A thought or a sentence for the day:

"What would you attempt to do if you knew you wouldn't fail?"
— **Anonymous**

MONTH 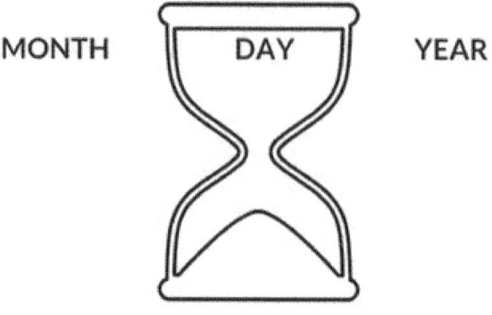 YEAR

This makes me happy:

A thought or a sentence for the day:

Live in the sunshine, swim in the sea, drink the wild air-
Ralph Waldon Emerson

A favorite seaside memory is:

"Two roads diverged in a wood and I – I took the one less traveled by." – Robert Frost

The most off-the-beaten-path adventure we had:

MONTH   DAY   YEAR

A thought or a sentence for the day:

If there is one thing I want to remember about this day it is this:

MONTH 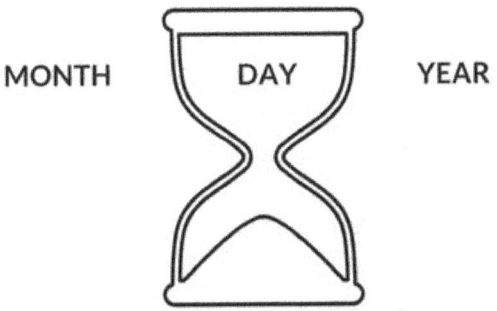 DAY   YEAR

If there is one thing I want to remember about this day it is this:

A thought or a sentence for the day:

| MONTH | DAY | YEAR |

A thought or a sentence for the day:

If there is one thing I want to remember about this day it is this:

MONTH 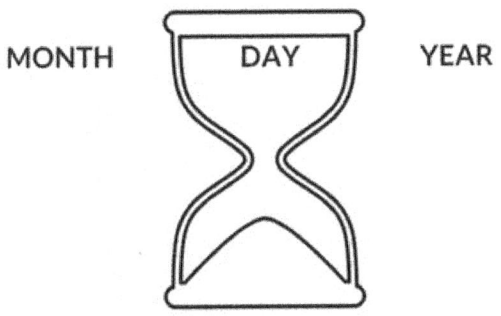 YEAR

Sometimes this makes me anxious:

A thought or a sentence for the day:

| MONTH | DAY | YEAR |

A thought or a sentence for the day:

If there is one thing I want to remember about this day it is this:

My favorite animal is:

(A list of the pets we had in 45 years)

Why does time seem to speed up with
each passing year?
This day feels like yesterday:

MONTH 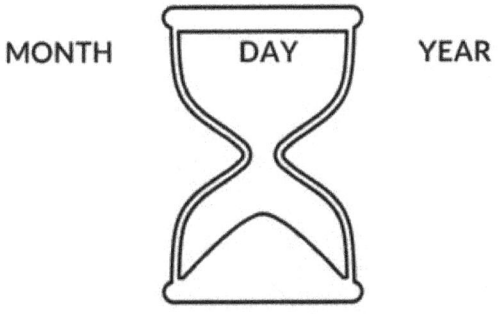 YEAR

The best book I've read this year or any year:

A thought or a sentence for the day:

MONTH DAY   YEAR

If there is one thing I want to remember about this day it is this:

A thought or a sentence for the day:

MONTH 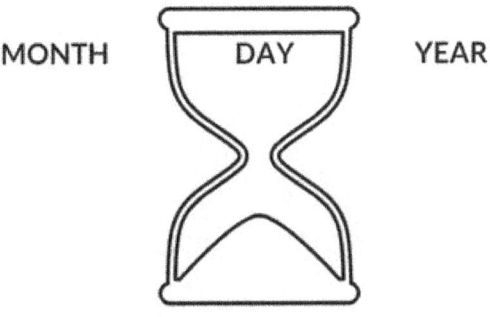 YEAR

I am most shocked by this:

A thought or a sentence for the day:

MONTH DAY   YEAR

If there is one thing I want to remember about this day it is this:

A thought or a sentence for the day:

MONTH 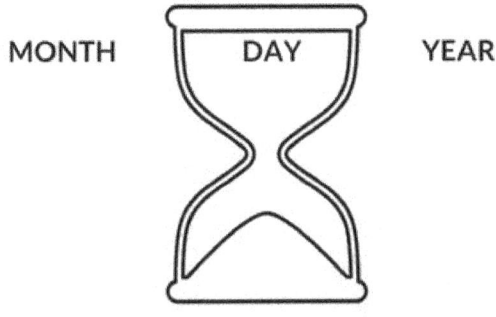 YEAR

I worry most about this:

A thought or a sentence for the day:

MONTH YEAR

If there is one thing I want to remember about this day it is this:

A thought or a sentence for the day:

MONTH YEAR

My favorite memory from my childhood:

A thought or a sentence for the day:

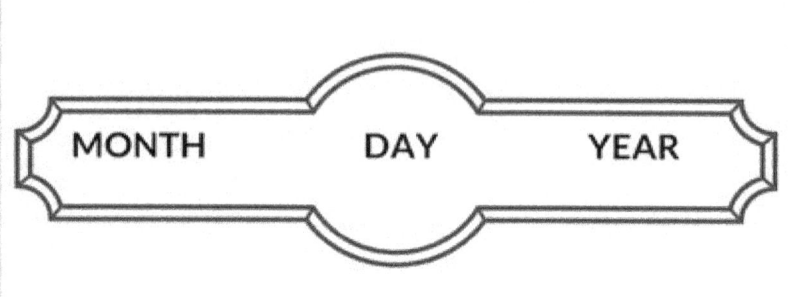

A thought or a sentence for the day:

If there is one thing I want to remember about this day it is this:

MONTH 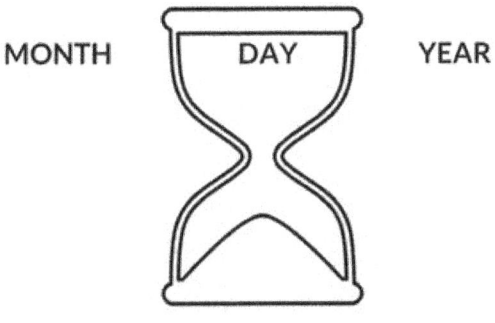 YEAR

I love this old song:

A thought or a sentence for the day:

Die with memories not dreams -unknown

MONTH 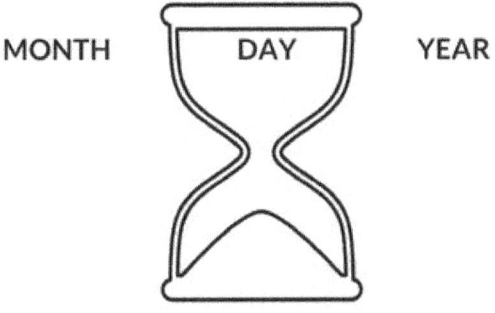 YEAR

If I had to pick my last meal:

A thought or a sentence for the day:

MONTH 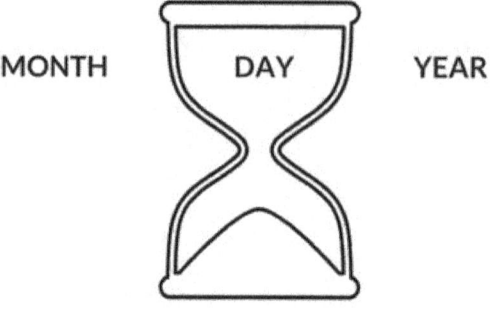 DAY   YEAR

If there is one thing I want to remember about this day it is this:

A thought or a sentence for the day:

MONTH 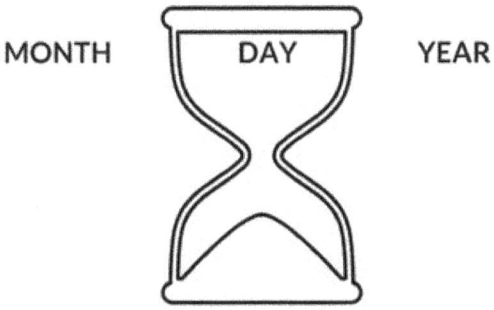 YEAR

If I could change one thing this year it would be:

A thought or a sentence for the day:

Sometimes we just need to say "Yes" more often...
This year I'm going to say yes to this:

| MONTH | DAY | YEAR |

A thought or a sentence for the day:

If there is one thing I want to remember about this day it is this:

MONTH 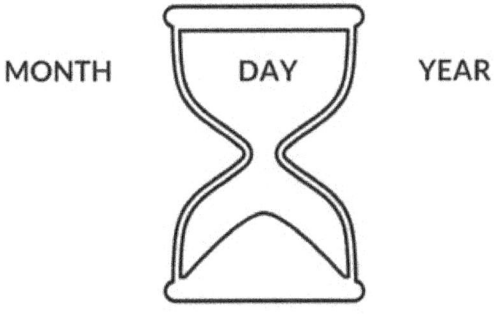 DAY YEAR

If there is one thing I want to remember about this day it is this:

A thought or a sentence for the day:

A great journey I will never forget:

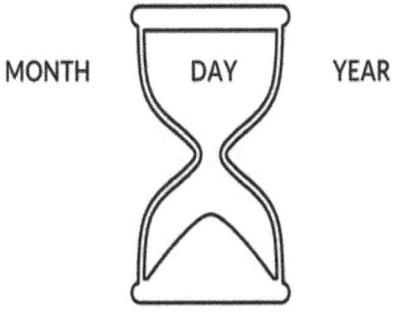

MONTH DAY YEAR

If there is one thing I want to remember about this day it is this:

A thought or a sentence for the day:

This year I have been busy with this:

MONTH 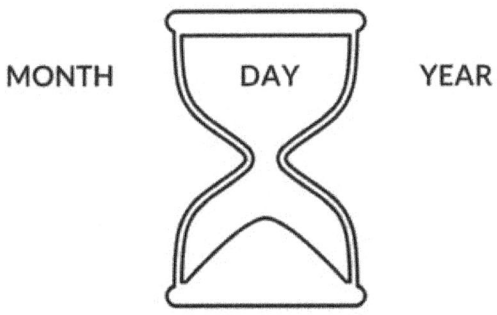 YEAR

If there is one thing I want to remember about this day it is this:

A thought or a sentence for the day:

Fill your life with adventures not things. Have stories to tell not to stuff to show.

A story of the moment I don't want to forget:

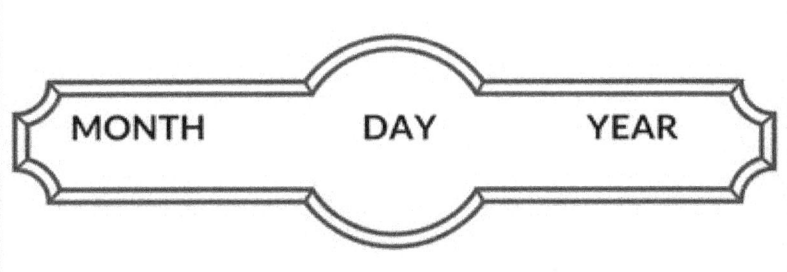

| MONTH | DAY | YEAR |

A thought or a sentence for the day:

If there is one thing I want to remember about this day it is this:

MONTH 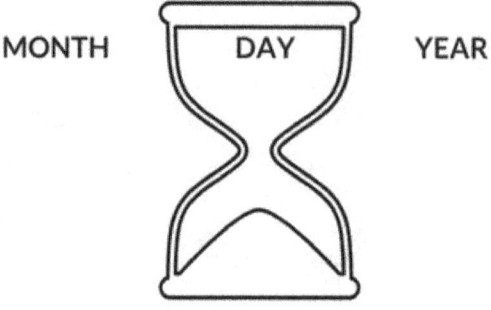 YEAR

When I think of my favorite
memory of my mother or father
it is this:

A thought or a sentence for the
day:

MONTH 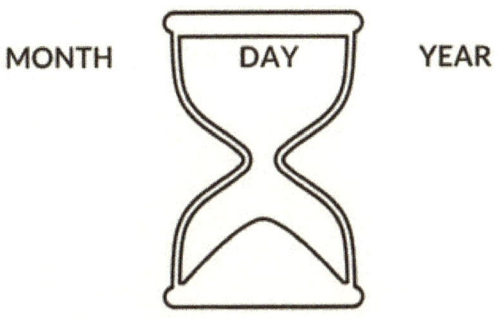 YEAR

This surprised me:

A thought or a sentence for the day:

MONTH 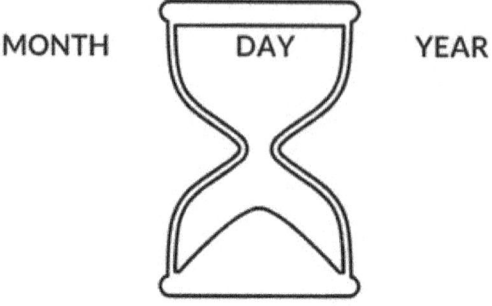 DAY YEAR

The most surprising event that happened this year in the world:

A thought or a sentence for the day:

MONTH 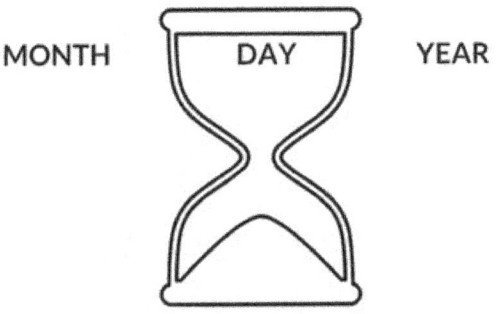 YEAR

I never thought I would see the day:

A thought or a sentence for the day:

MONTH 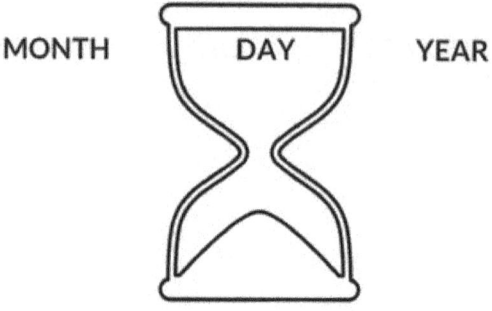 YEAR

When I think of my biggest accomplishment this year:

A thought or a sentence for the day:

MONTH 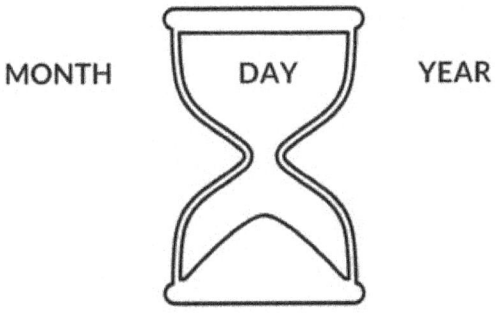 YEAR

DAY

If there is one thing I want to remember about this day it is this:

A thought or a sentence for the day:

"Life is either a daring adventure or nothing." -- Helen Keller

One of my favorite adventures this year:

MONTH YEAR

If there is one thing I want to remember about this day it is this:

A thought or a sentence for the day:

MONTH DAY YEAR

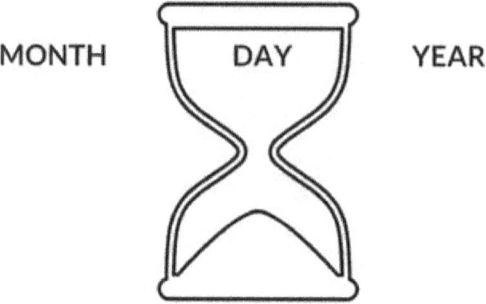

Things that make me wonder:

A thought or a sentence for the day:

MONTH 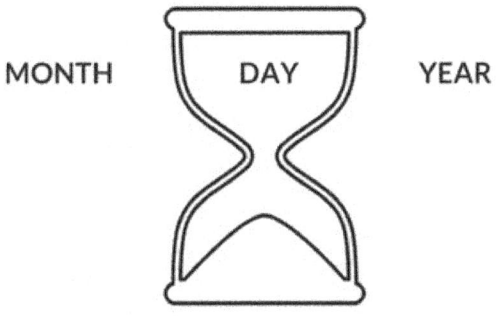 YEAR

If there is one thing I want to remember about this day it is this:

A thought or a sentence for the day:

| MONTH | DAY | YEAR |

A thought or a sentence for the day:

If there is one thing I want to remember about this day it is this:

MONTH 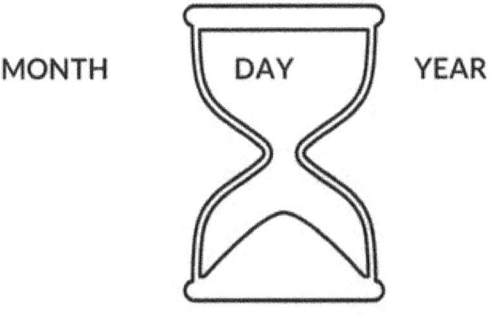 YEAR

I loved this movie:

A thought or a sentence for the day:

This was a funny moment of our 45 years:

We didn't realize this would go on for Forty-five years, my aren't we surprised.

One of my favorite memories from meeting you:

The first day we met:

MONTH 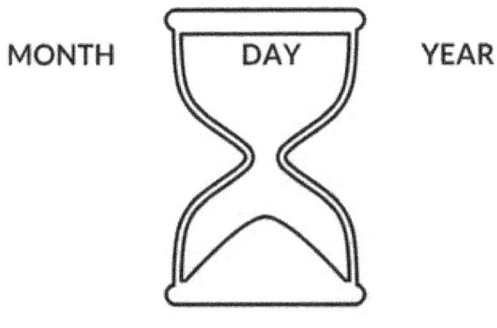 YEAR

I can't believe:

A thought or a sentence for the day:

MONTH   DAY   YEAR

A thought or a sentence for the day:

If there is one thing I want to remember about this day it is this:

MONTH 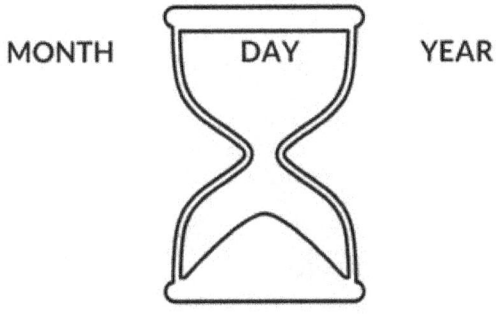 YEAR

I will remember this year for:

A thought or a sentence for the day:

MONTH 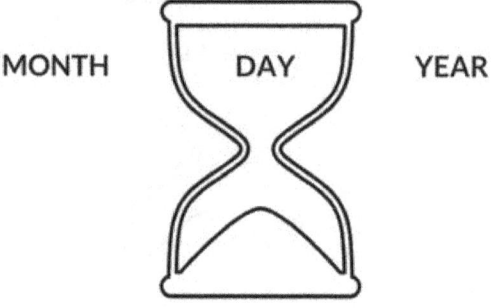 DAY YEAR

If there is one thing I want to remember about this day it is this:

A thought or a sentence for the day:

MONTH 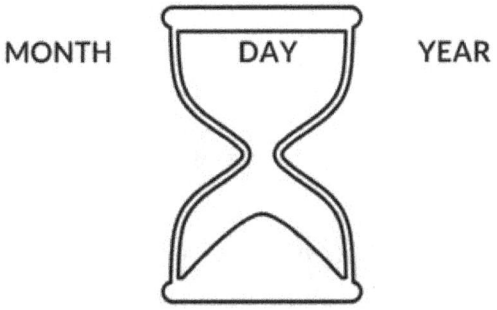 YEAR

At this point in my life, this is my best advice for someone I love:

A thought or a sentence for the day:

The world is big, and I want to get a good look at it before it gets dark. - John Muir

MONTH DAY   YEAR

If there is one thing I want to remember about this day it is this:

A thought or a sentence for the day:

MONTH YEAR

I never want to forget:

A thought or a sentence for the day:

MONTH DAY YEAR

A thought or a sentence for the day:

If there is one thing I want to remember about this day it is this:

MONTH　　DAY　　YEAR

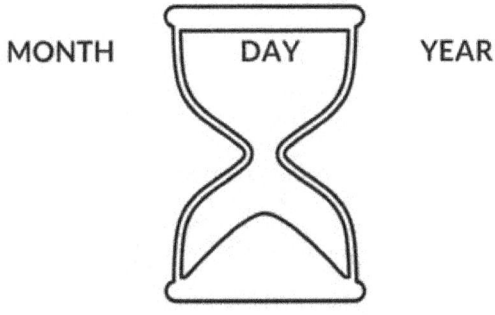

The food I can't stand:

A thought or a sentence for the day:

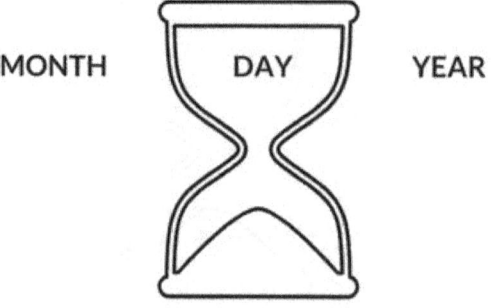

MONTH   DAY   YEAR

If there is one thing I want to remember about this day it is this:

A thought or a sentence for the day:

MONTH 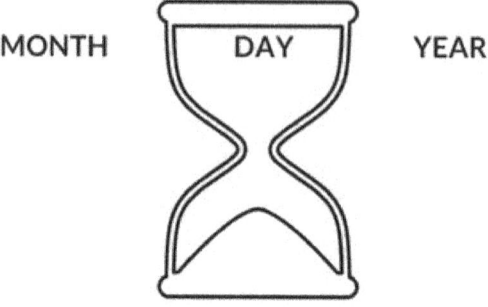 YEAR

I love this season best of all:

A thought or a sentence for the day:

MONTH DAY YEAR

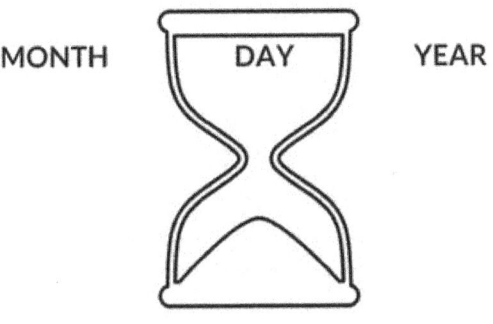

This surprised me:

A thought or a sentence for the day:

MONTH DAY YEAR

My favorite memory from my childhood:

A thought or a sentence for the day:

MONTH 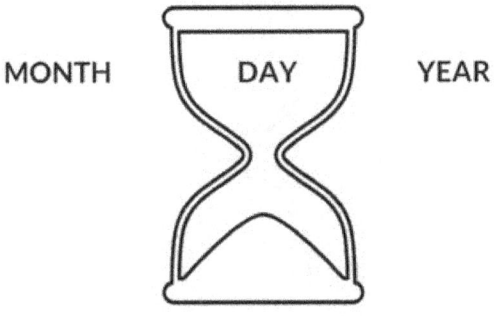 DAY   YEAR

If there is one thing I want to remember about this day it is this:

A thought or a sentence for the day:

MONTH DAY   YEAR

If there is one thing I want to remember about this day it is this:

A thought or a sentence for the day:

MONTH 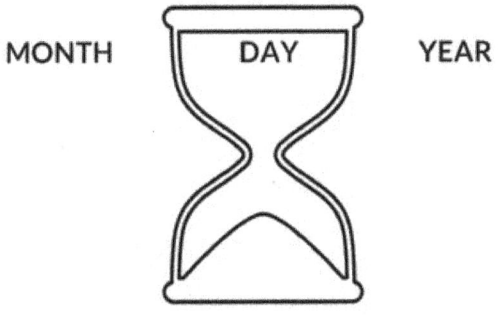 YEAR

I never want to forget:

A thought or a sentence for the day:

MONTH 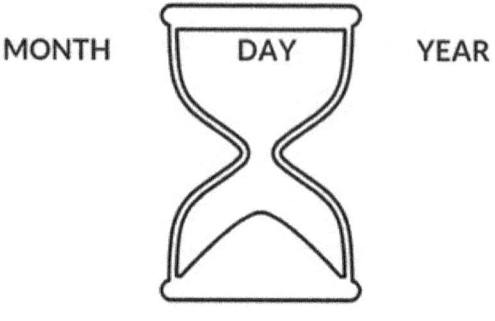 YEAR

I wish I could:

A thought or a sentence for the day:

MONTH 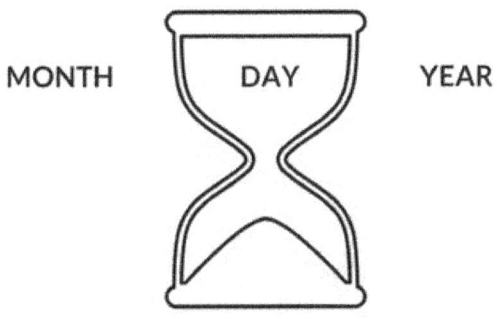 YEAR

If there is one thing I want to remember about this day it is this:

A thought or a sentence for the day:

If I won an all-expense-paid vacation, I would go to:

MONTH   DAY   YEAR

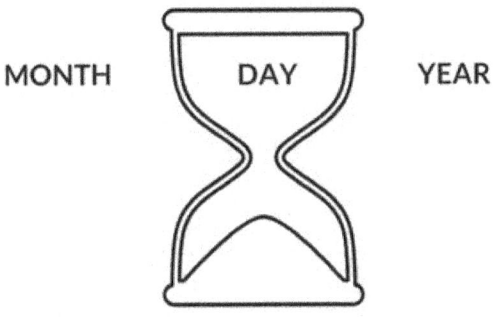

If there is one thing I want to remember about this day it is this:

A thought or a sentence for the day:

MONTH 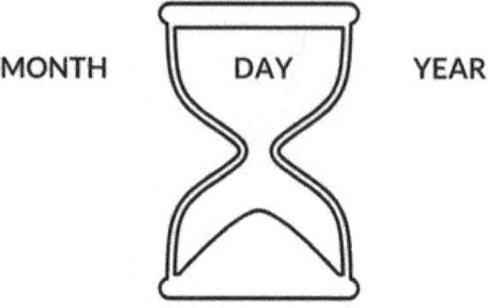 DAY   YEAR

If there is one thing I want to remember about this day it is this:

A thought or a sentence for the day:

MONTH DAY YEAR

A thought or a sentence for the day:

If there is one thing I want to remember about this day it is this:

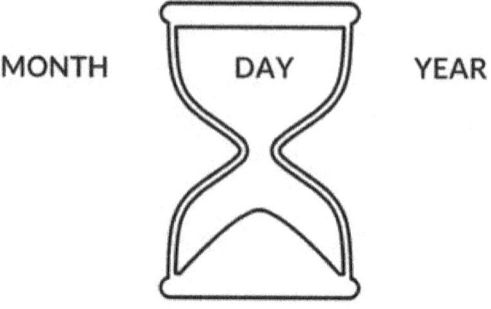

MONTH   DAY   YEAR

If there is one thing I want to remember about this day it is this:

A thought or a sentence for the day:

MONTH 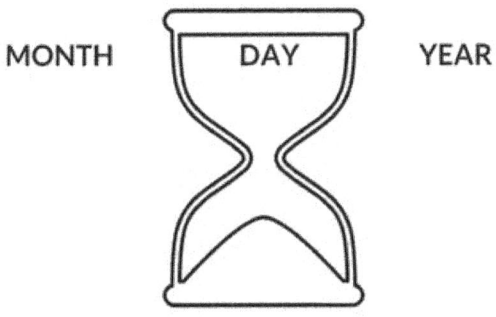 YEAR

I never want to forget:

A thought or a sentence for the day:

MONTH DAY   YEAR

If there is one thing I want to remember about this day it is this:

A thought or a sentence for the day:

MONTH   DAY   YEAR

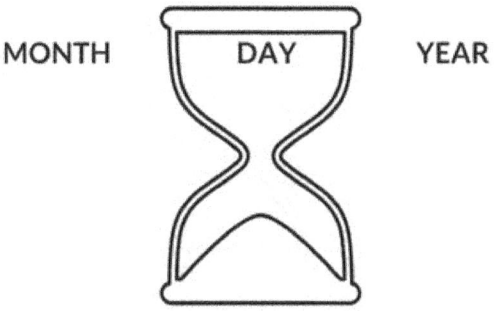

My pet peeve of the moment:

A thought or a sentence for the day:

MONTH 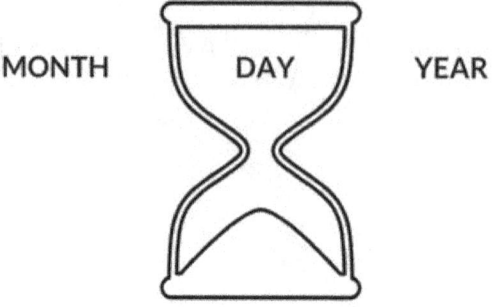 DAY   YEAR

If there is one thing I want to remember about this day it is this:

A thought or a sentence for the day:

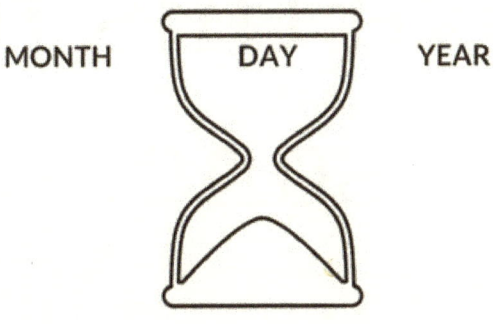

I love this old song:

A thought or a sentence for the day:

I love this new song:

One of the best Vacations Ever:

MONTH   DAY   YEAR

A thought or a sentence for the day:

If there is one thing I want to remember about this day it is this:

MONTH 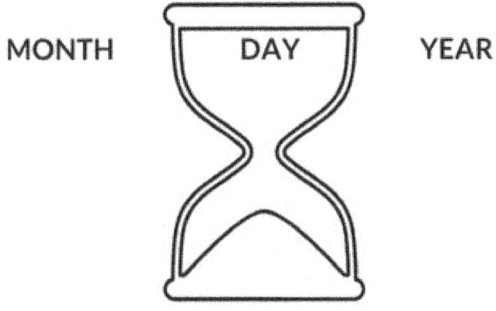 YEAR

Right now my favorite vacation was:

A thought or a sentence for the day:

MONTH 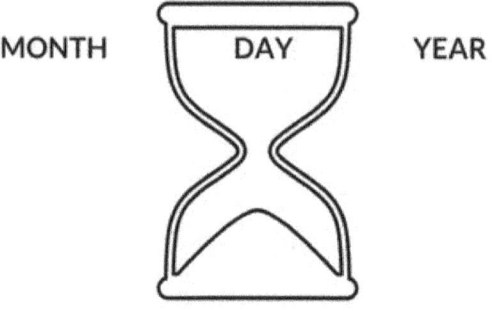 YEAR

When I think of my favorite
memory of my mother or father
it is this:

A thought or a sentence for the
day:

MONTH 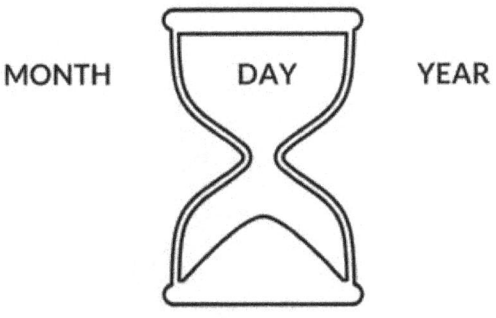 DAY   YEAR

If there is one thing I want to remember about this day it is this:

A thought or a sentence for the day:

MONTH 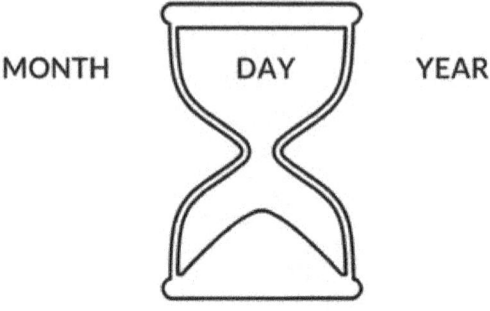 DAY YEAR

If there is one thing I want to remember about this day it is this:

A thought or a sentence for the day:

MONTH 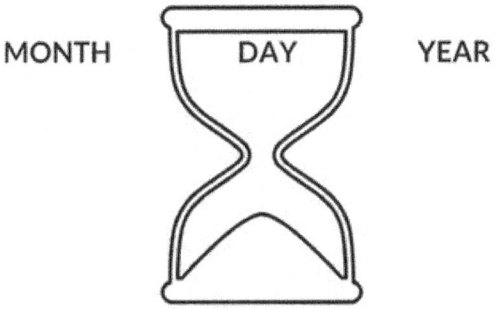 YEAR

At this point in my life, this is my best advice for someone I love:

A thought or a sentence for the day:

MONTH 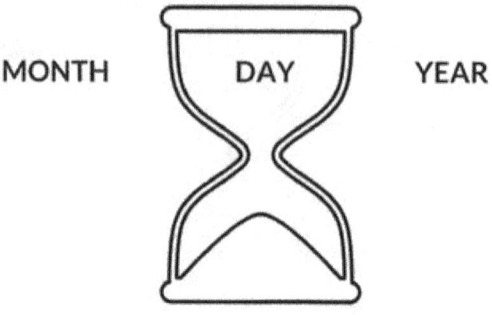 DAY   YEAR

If there is one thing I want to remember about this day it is this:

A thought or a sentence for the day:

MONTH YEAR

Things that make me wonder:

A thought or a sentence for the day:

MONTH   DAY   YEAR

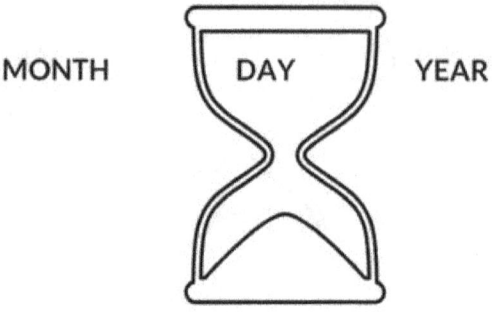

I loved this movie:

A thought or a sentence for the day:

MONTH   DAY   YEAR

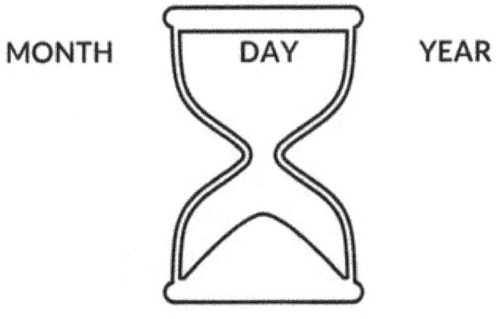

I never want to forget:

A thought or a sentence for the day:

MONTH DAY   YEAR

If there is one thing I want to remember about this day it is this:

A thought or a sentence for the day:

I need more of this:

MONTH DAY   YEAR

If there is one thing I want to remember about this day it is this:

A thought or a sentence for the day:

I dream of this place:

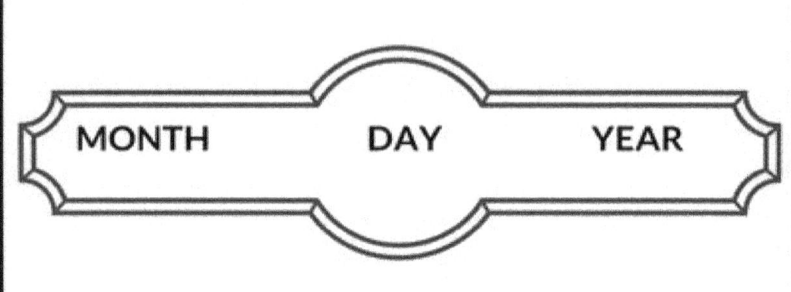

A thought or a sentence for the day:

If there is one thing I want to remember about this day it is this:

A thought or a sentence for the day:

If there is one thing I want to remember about this day it is this:

MONTH 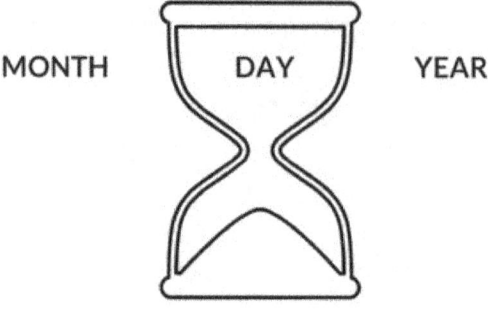 DAY   YEAR

If there is one thing I want to remember about this day it is this:

A thought or a sentence for the day:

MONTH 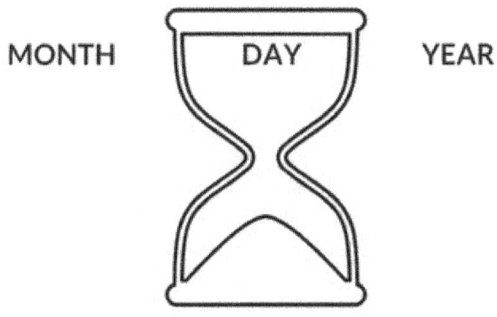 YEAR

I will remember this year for:

A thought or a sentence for the day:

MONTH 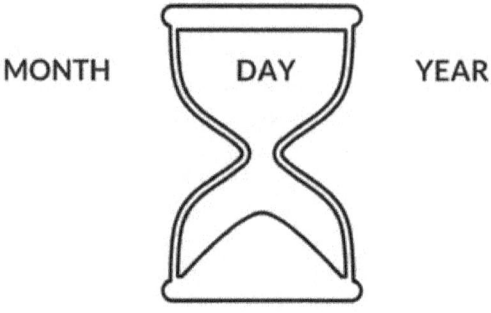 DAY   YEAR

If there is one thing I want to remember about this day it is this:

A thought or a sentence for the day:

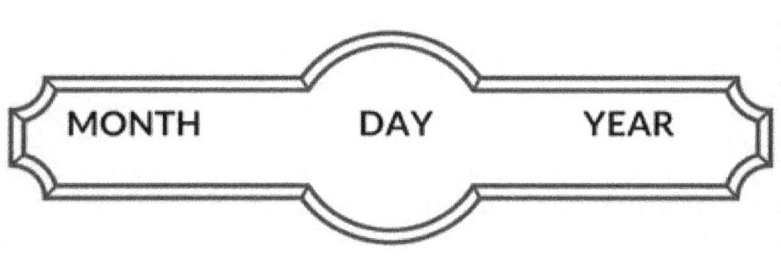

A thought or a sentence for the day:

If there is one thing I want to remember about this day it is this:

MONTH 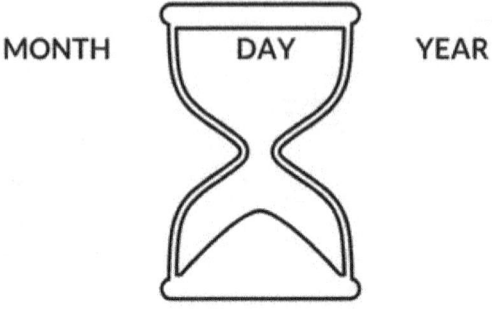 YEAR

I can't believe:

A thought or a sentence for the day:

MONTH 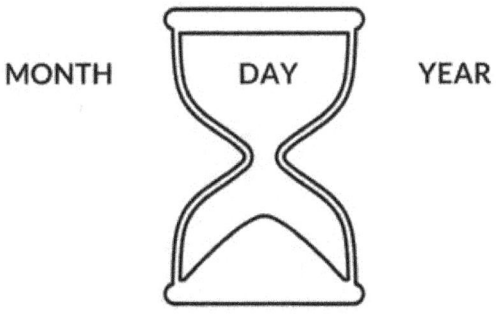 DAY   YEAR

If there is one thing I want to remember about this day it is this:

A thought or a sentence for the day:

MONTH   DAY   YEAR

If there is one thing I want to remember about this day it is this:

A thought or a sentence for the day:

MONTH 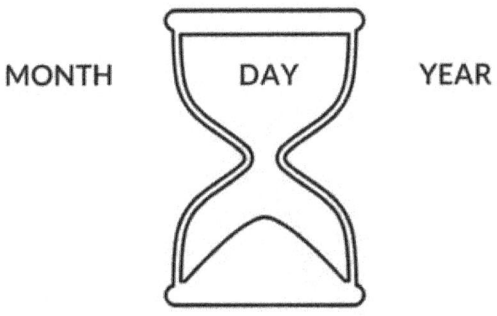 YEAR

DAY

If there is one thing I want to remember about this day it is this:

A thought or a sentence for the day:

MONTH 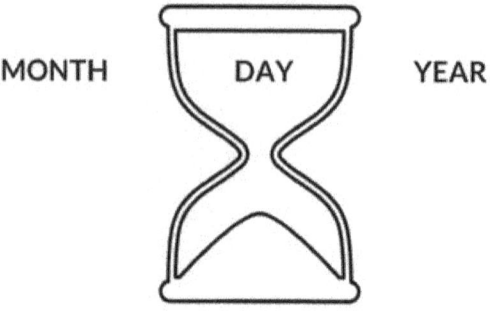 DAY   YEAR

If there is one thing I want to remember about this day it is this:

A thought or a sentence for the day:

MONTH 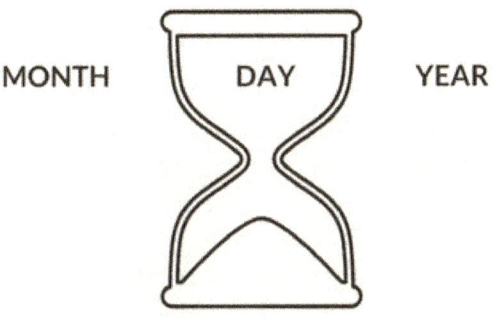 YEAR

If there is one thing I want to remember about this day it is this:

A thought or a sentence for the day:

A thought or a sentence for the day:

If there is one thing I want to remember about this day it is this:

MONTH 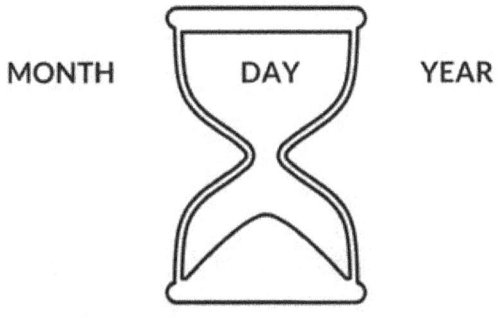 YEAR

If there is one thing I want to remember about this day it is this:

A thought or a sentence for the day:

Always take the scenic route makes me think of:

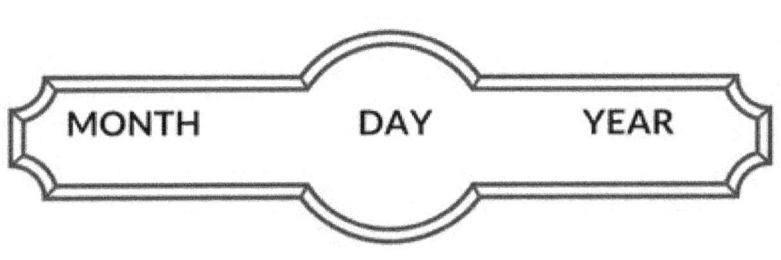

A thought or a sentence for the day:

If there is one thing I want to remember about this day it is this:

MONTH 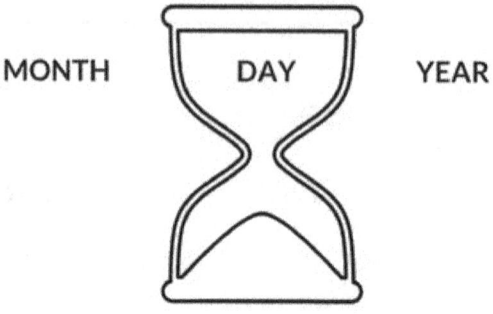 YEAR

If there is one thing I want to remember about this day it is this:

A thought or a sentence for the day:

MONTH 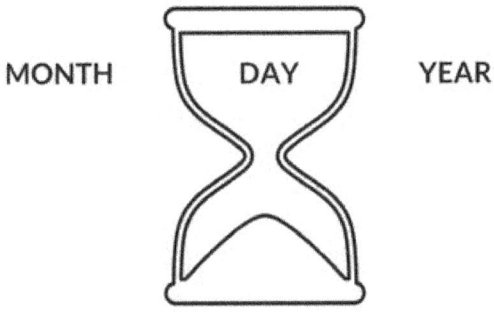 DAY   YEAR

If there is one thing I want to remember about this day it is this:

A thought or a sentence for the day:

A thought or a sentence for the day:

If there is one thing I want to remember about this day it is this:

A lesson I learned as a child:

A few of my favorite things:

MONTH 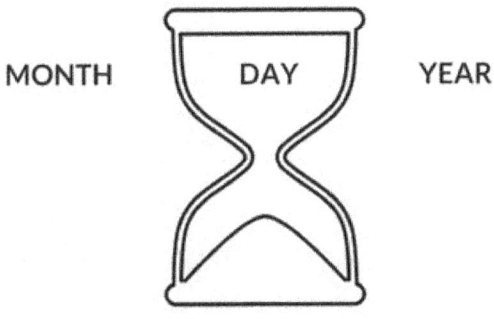 DAY   YEAR

If there is one thing I want to remember about this day it is this:

A thought or a sentence for the day:

We really wanted to name our kids:

MONTH 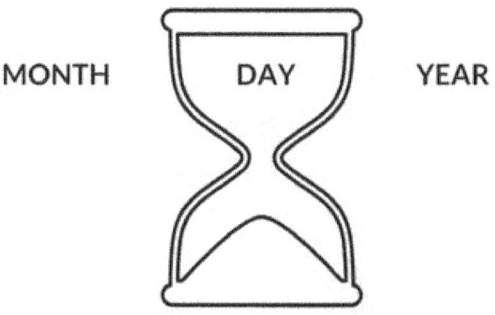 DAY　　　YEAR

If there is one thing I want to remember about this day it is this:

A thought or a sentence for the day:

MONTH DAY YEAR

If there is one thing I want to remember about this day it is this:

A thought or a sentence for the day:

MONTH 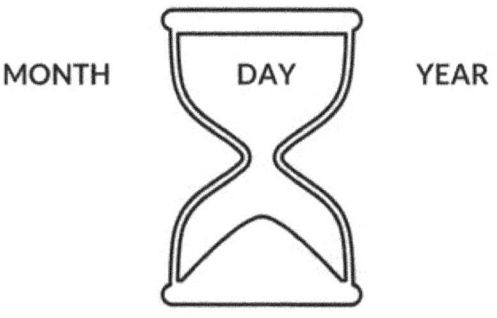 DAY   YEAR

If there is one thing I want to remember about this day it is this:

A thought or a sentence for the day:

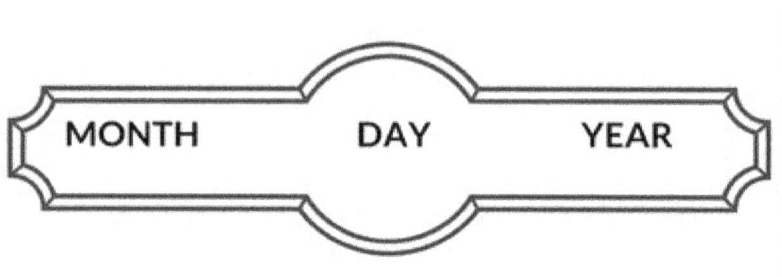

MONTH   DAY   YEAR

A thought or a sentence for the day:

If there is one thing I want to remember about this day it is this:

| MONTH | DAY | YEAR |

A thought or a sentence for the day:

If there is one thing I want to remember about this day it is this:

Top five movies we love:

Top five foods from the past we crave:

Top five bands we love:

Top five TV shows we love:

MONTH 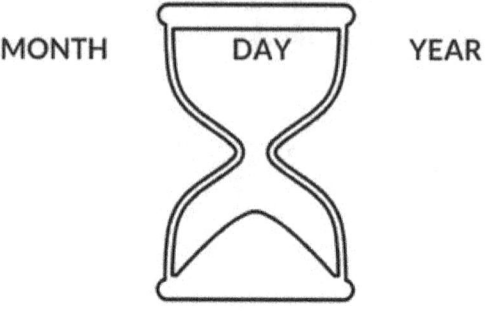 YEAR

I will remember this year for:

A thought or a sentence for the day:

MONTH 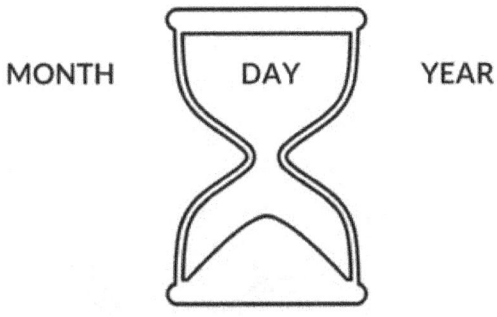 YEAR

If there is one thing I want to remember about this day it is this:

A thought or a sentence for the day:

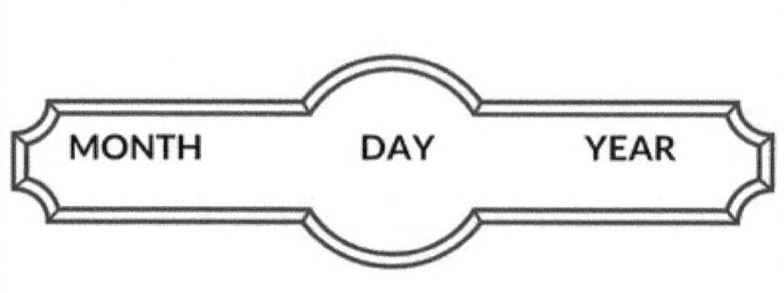

| MONTH | DAY | YEAR |

A thought or a sentence for the day:

If there is one thing I want to remember about this day it is this:

MONTH   DAY   YEAR

A thought or a sentence for the day:

If there is one thing I want to remember about this day it is this:

Love is not about how many days, months, or years, you have been together. Love is about how much you love each other every single day.
-unknown

My favorite thing about being married is:

When we get to the end of
our lives together, the house
we had, the cars we drove,
the things we possessed
won't matter. What will
matter is that I had you,
and you had me.
-unknown
I love this about you:

MONTH 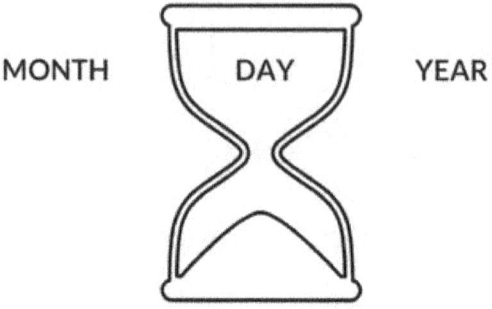 DAY YEAR

If there is one thing I want to remember about this day it is this:

A thought or a sentence for the day:

MONTH 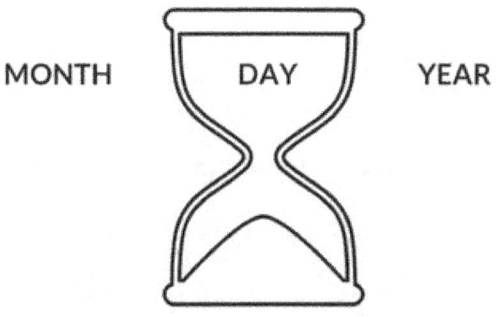 YEAR

If there is one thing I want to remember about this day it is this:

A thought or a sentence for the day:

Love is patient, love is kind. Love does not envy, it does not boast, it is not proud. It does not dishonor others, it is not self-seeking, it is not easily angered, it keeps no record of wrongs. Love does not delight in evil but rejoices with the truth. It always protects, always trusts, always hopes, always perseveres....1 Corinthians 13

I hope I never forget:

MONTH   DAY   YEAR

A thought or a sentence for the day:

If there is one thing I want to remember about this day it is this:

MONTH   DAY   YEAR

A thought or a sentence for the day:

If there is one thing I want to remember about this day it is this:

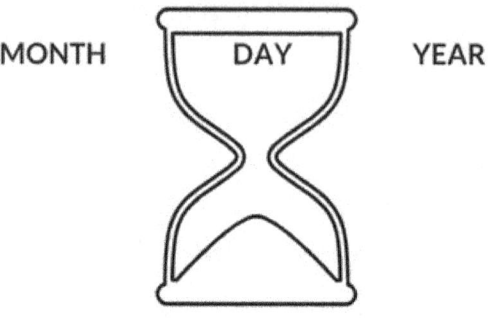

MONTH   DAY   YEAR

I can't believe:

A thought or a sentence for the day:

MONTH 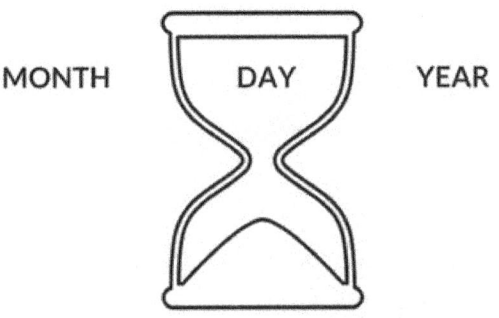 YEAR

If there is one thing I want to remember about this day it is this:

A thought or a sentence for the day:

MONTH 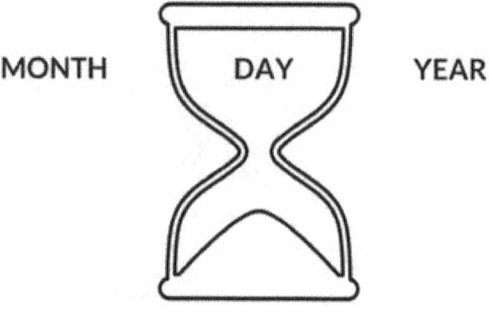 DAY   YEAR

If there is one thing I want to remember about this day it is this:

A thought or a sentence for the day:

MONTH 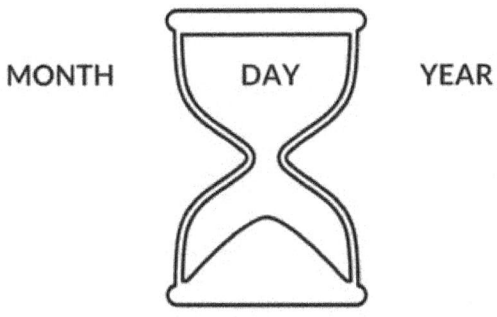 YEAR

If there is one thing I want to remember about this day it is this:

A thought or a sentence for the day:

MONTH 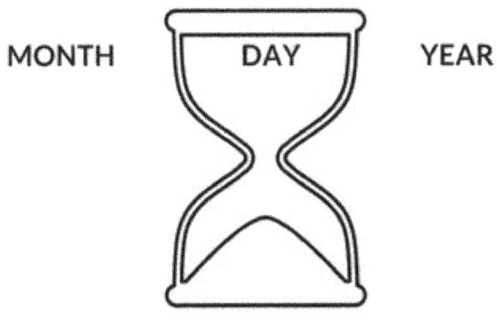 YEAR

I never want to forget:

A thought or a sentence for the day:

Remember

When?

Anniversary editions available on Amazon:
1st Anniversary: One Epic Year
5th Anniversary: Five Epic Years
10th Anniversary: Ten Epic Years
15th Anniversary: Fifteen Epic Years
20th Anniversary: Twenty Epic Years
25th Anniversary: Twenty-five Epic Years
30th Anniversary: Thirty Epic Years
35th Anniversary: Thirty-five Epic Years
40th Anniversary: Forty Epic Years
45th Anniversary: Forty-five Epic Years
50th Anniversary: Fifty Epic Years

Perfect Anniversary Gift

Books With Soul

Books with Soul believes in sharing gifts that inspire and motivate
others to create memories and keep a record of the story of their life.

What if… you had a record of your memories or someone you loved?

INSPIRATION COMES IN ALL SIZES, SHAPES AND IDEAS

WE believe every life is worth a few written words to pass on or reflect on in the future.
You don't have to be an author to tell the story of your life. Just be you.
Today will someday be the good old days, remember them.
Books with Soul offers inspirational journals with questions and thoughts to help record memories for the most novice of journalers, great birthday, milestone, wedding and baby gifts. Help someone write their life story.

Questions? Email info@bookswithsoul.com
We appreciate every reader, every traveler and recorder of history.
We would love if you took the time to write a
review on Amazon and let us know if the books motivated you.

Find more journals, inspiration, diaries, coloring books and gifts for every milestone at:
www.bookswithsoul.com

If you would like to have a personalized journal for
an organization, company,
group, club,
or activity, contact
Books with Soul.
Special unique journals in 25 quantities or more can
be created.

*if someone bought you this journal, pay it forward and buy a journal
for someone
you care about.
Help them write the story of their life.

Books with Soul ™

was inspired from a lover of music and life, who believed in the soul. He had a collection of wonderful things. Physical memories you could read, touch, and listen to- including thousands of vinyl albums. Old school music, that lasts forever. In 2018, he passed away from brain cancer, but his memory lives on as others go old school. Collect pieces of your history, put pencil to paper, and record written memories. A physical book will not be lost in the cloud, and will last longer than a lifetime.

Keep a record of the story of your life. Your Words. Your Pages.

This is for you Mark.

www.ingramcontent.com/pod-product-compliance
Lightning Source LLC
Chambersburg PA
CBHW022114040426
42450CB00006B/699